The Dove

Friedrich Recknagel and Vlasta Baránková

Translated by Alison Sage

HUTCHINSON
London   Melbourne   Auckland   Johannesburg

A long time ago, a wise king ruled over a broad and beautiful country called Goldenland. Nearby was another kingdom, exactly the same size and just as lovely, called Silverland. The two kings were good friends and, although their palaces were far apart, they would often send each other messages by dove.

One summer, whilst the king of Silverland's son was staying with the king of Goldenland, the swiftest dove arrived, proudly carrying a royal message.

'My own dove!' cried the king's son, as he opened the letter. Then his face fell: his father was dead and he was now the new king.

The new king tried to rule wisely, as his father had done, but he had many new advisers and some were neither wise nor kind. 'That daft old fool,' they said, speaking of his father's old friend, 'how does he dare to call his kingdom Goldenland? It is an insult to your dear father's memory.'

The young king began to listen to them and, before long, he had sent an angry message to the king of Goldenland. 'If you do not change the name of your country to Ironland within seven days, I shall send my armies to destroy you.'

The king of Goldenland called a meeting. 'Can we beat them?' he asked.

'Maybe we can,' said his ministers, 'but then, again, maybe we can't.'

The king sat in thought for a long while. Finally he said, 'Our land is the same, whatever it is called. How can I kill our people for the sake of a name?' He wrote: 'We have always been friends, not enemies. Why should a name come between us? We shall call our country Ironland as you ask.'

The prime minister looked anxious. 'We only have seven days. How can we send a message in that short a time?'

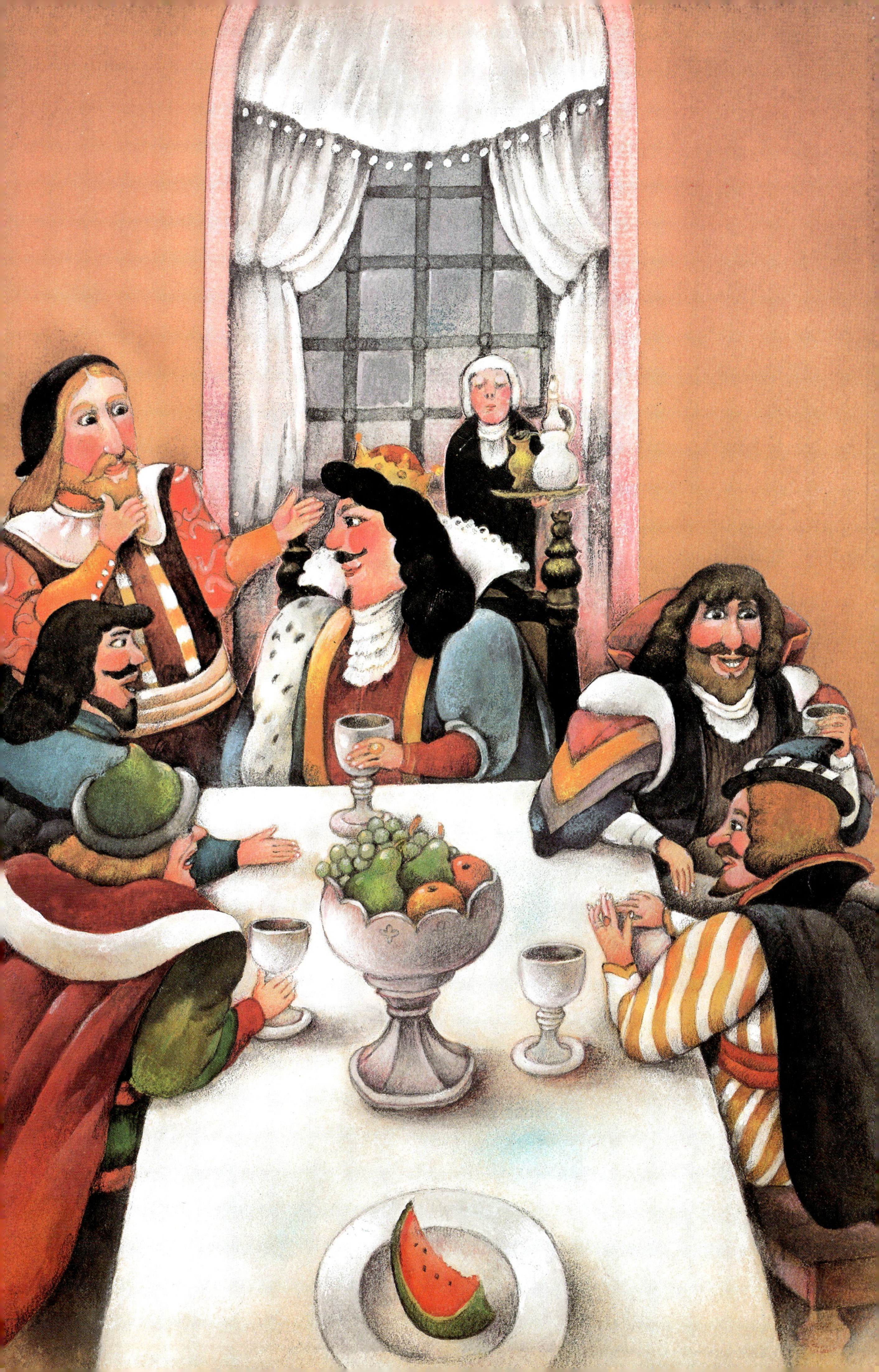

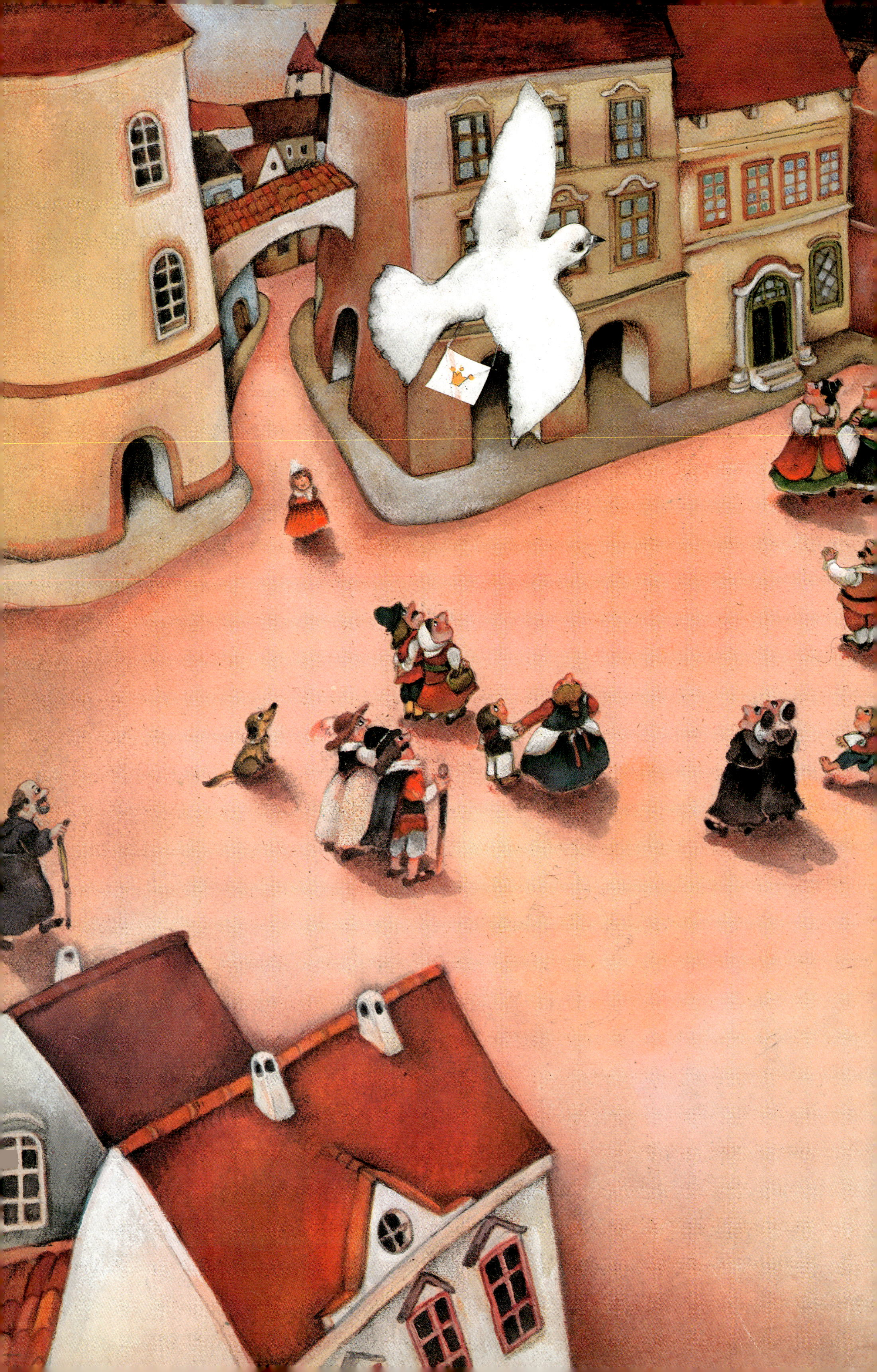

Then the king remembered the swift white dove which had brought the news of his friend's death. He sealed the message with the Royal Seal and, tying it to the dove's leg he said, 'Fly as fast as you can, dear bird. You are our only hope.'

The dove shot into the air like an arrow, her wings beating in the wind. She spiralled upwards, delighted to be free, then she headed south for Silverland.

By evening she had reached the seashore.
 'A white dove,' creaked the alligators in surprise. 'What brings you here in such a hurry?'
 'I am flying to stop a war,' said the dove, proudly. 'I have only six days left.'

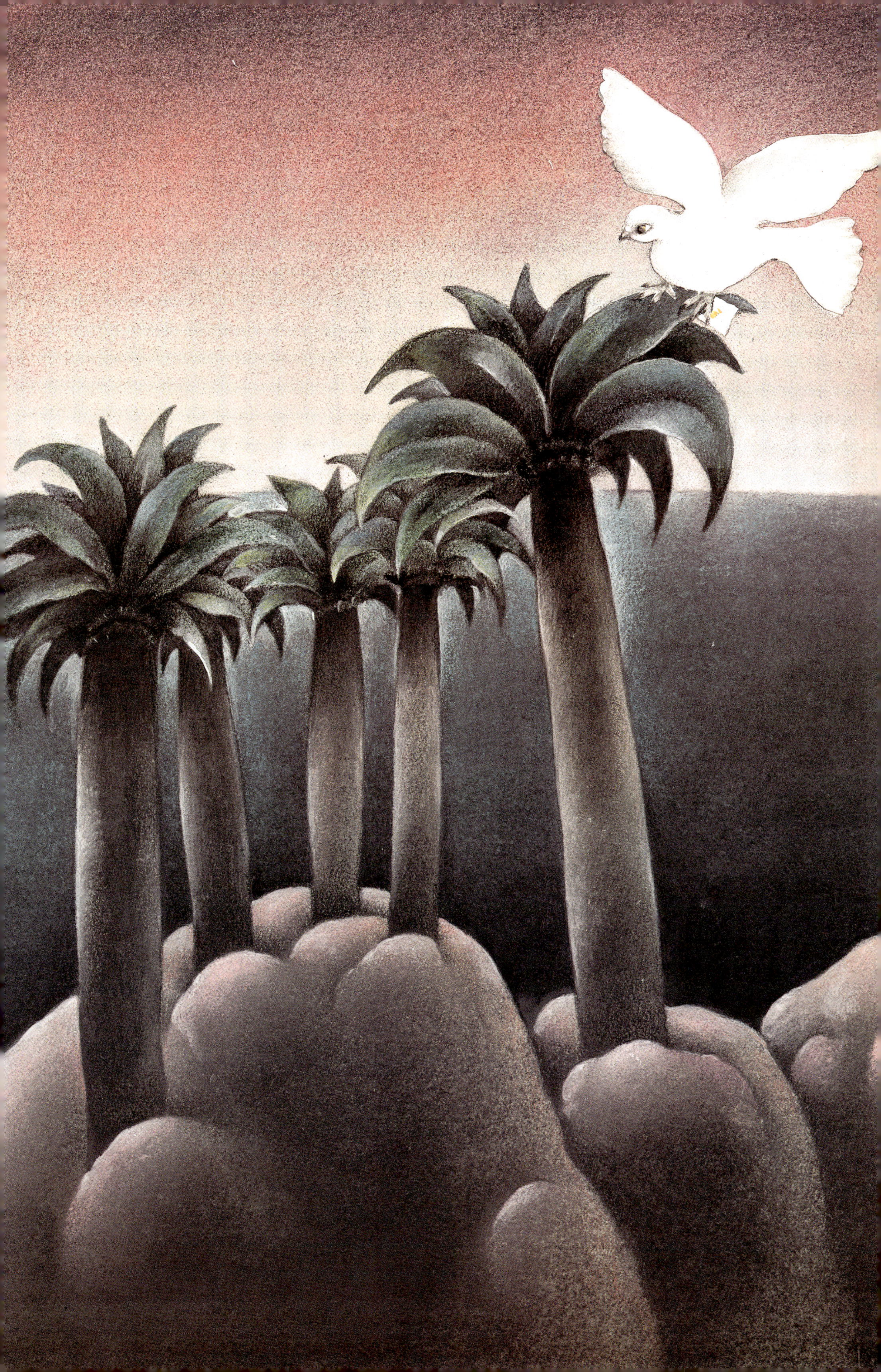

Before dawn, the dove was on her way; but daylight never came. It grew darker and darker. Lightning crackled in the heavy clouds and soon the sea turned frothy with wind-driven rain. Then the storm passed, but the dove was very tired. Gratefully, she fluttered down to rest on an uprooted tree that bobbed up and down on the waves.

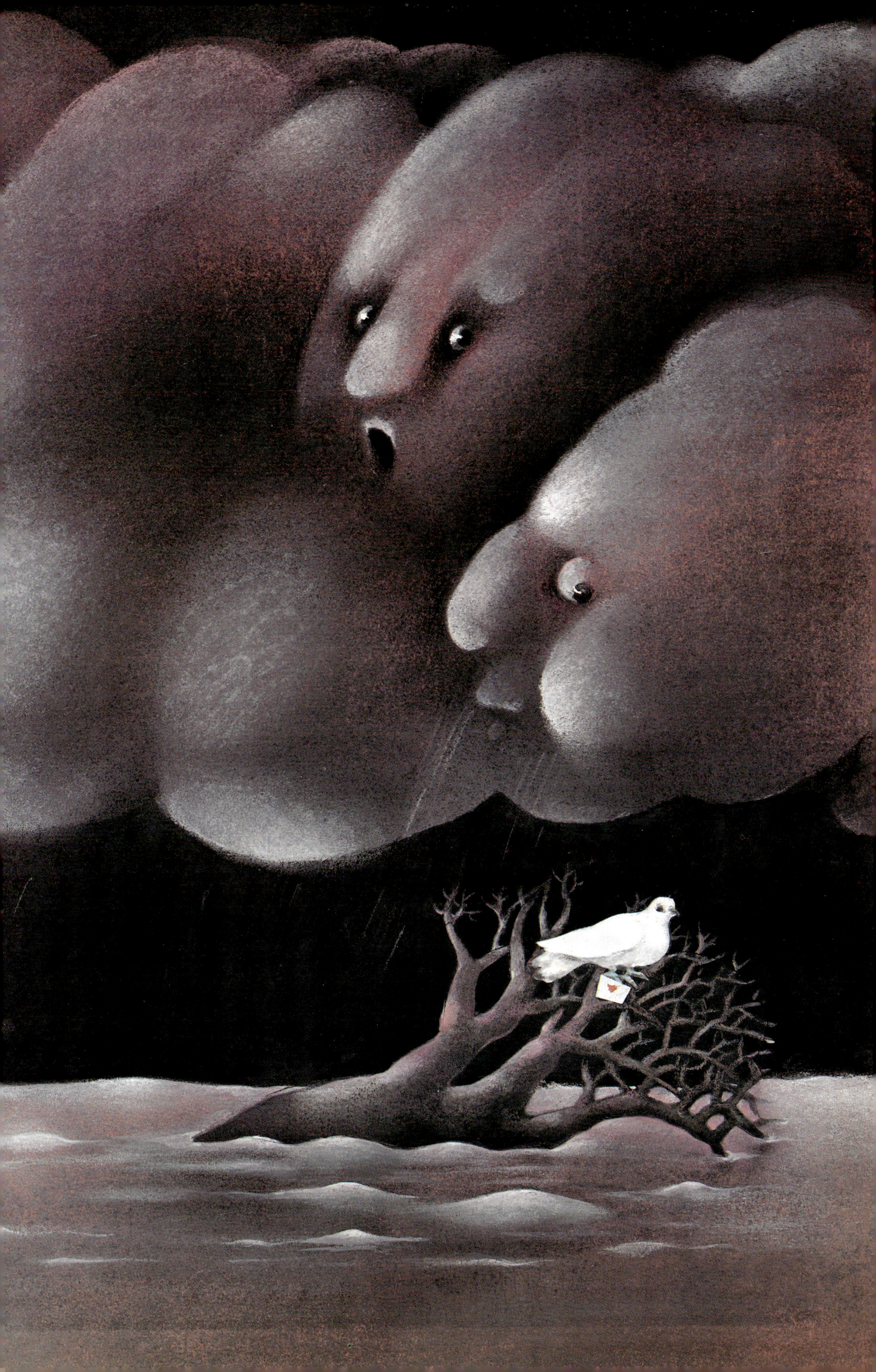

Morning came on the third day and the dove flew on. The storm had blown her far out of her way and she had many extra miles to go. Then she saw the seashore and her heart beat faster with excitement: it must be the coast of Silverland. She landed; but the beach was full of soldiers. 'We shall sail in four days,' ordered the commander.

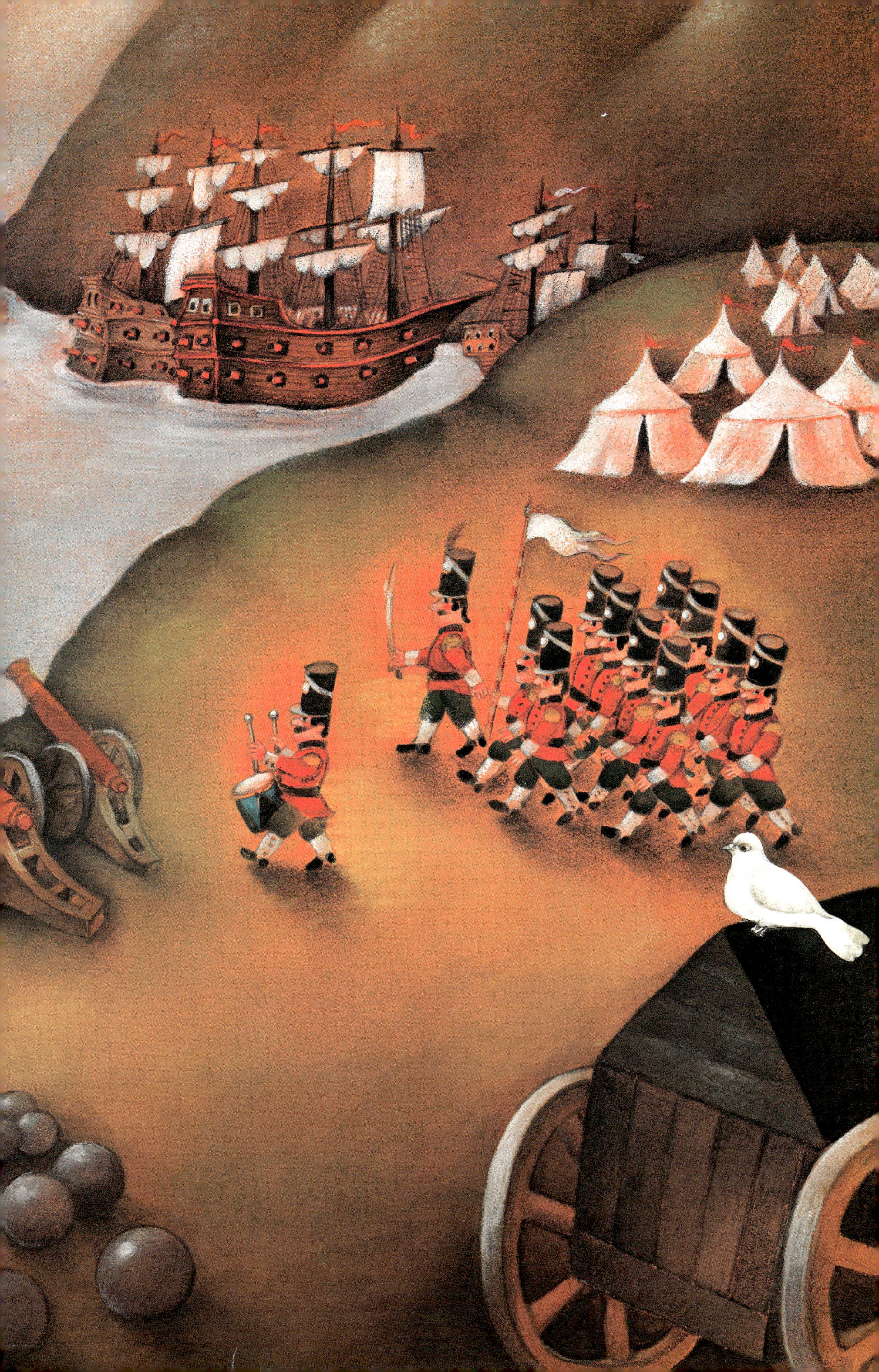

After a few hours' rest, the dove set off again. She still had the mountains to cross. The air was cold and still and, below her, the mountain tops glittered with ice. She was hungry, but there was no food on the bare rock and she dared not stop. Grey shadows closed around her as night began to fall; but now the steep mountains had smoothed into hill slopes and, exhausted, she perched on an old tree and slept.

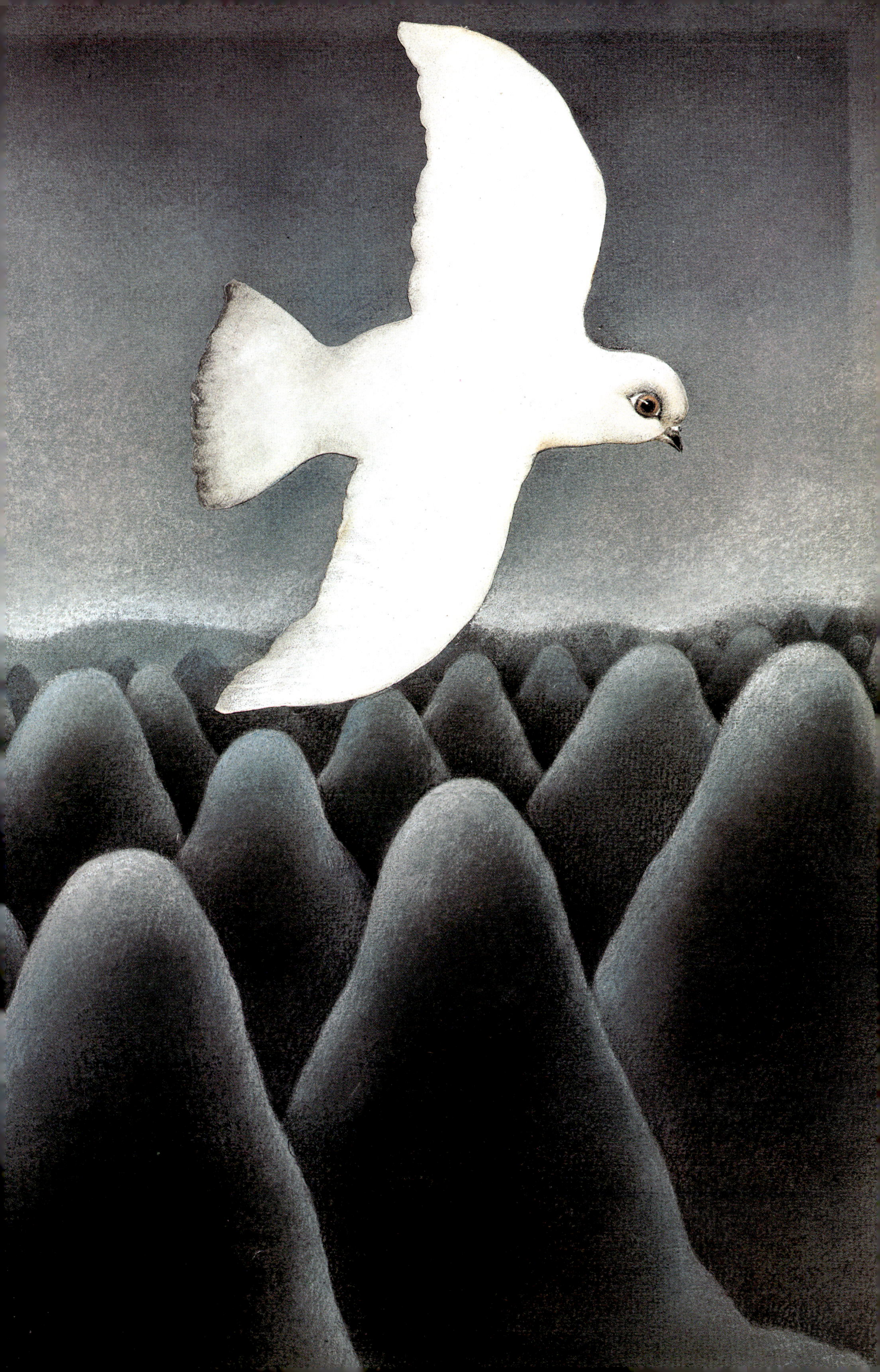

On the fifth day, she was hardly able to open her eyes. Feebly, she flapped her wings, but she had no strength left.

Then, 'Look,' said a gentle voice, 'there's a poor, tired bird. It can't even fly.' And a small boy came running across the field. 'What's the matter, little one?' he asked, lifting up the dove and stroking her.

'Hungry, I expect. And cold, too,' said his sister. 'Give her some of our bread.'

Eagerly, the dove pecked the crumbs of food.

'Let's take her home,' said the girl.

'She can sleep in our bed,' said her brother.

The dove nestled against his shoulder. It was good to rest.

She woke the next morning before it was light and sadly she flew round the children's bed. She knew she must leave them and fly onwards. She had only two days left.

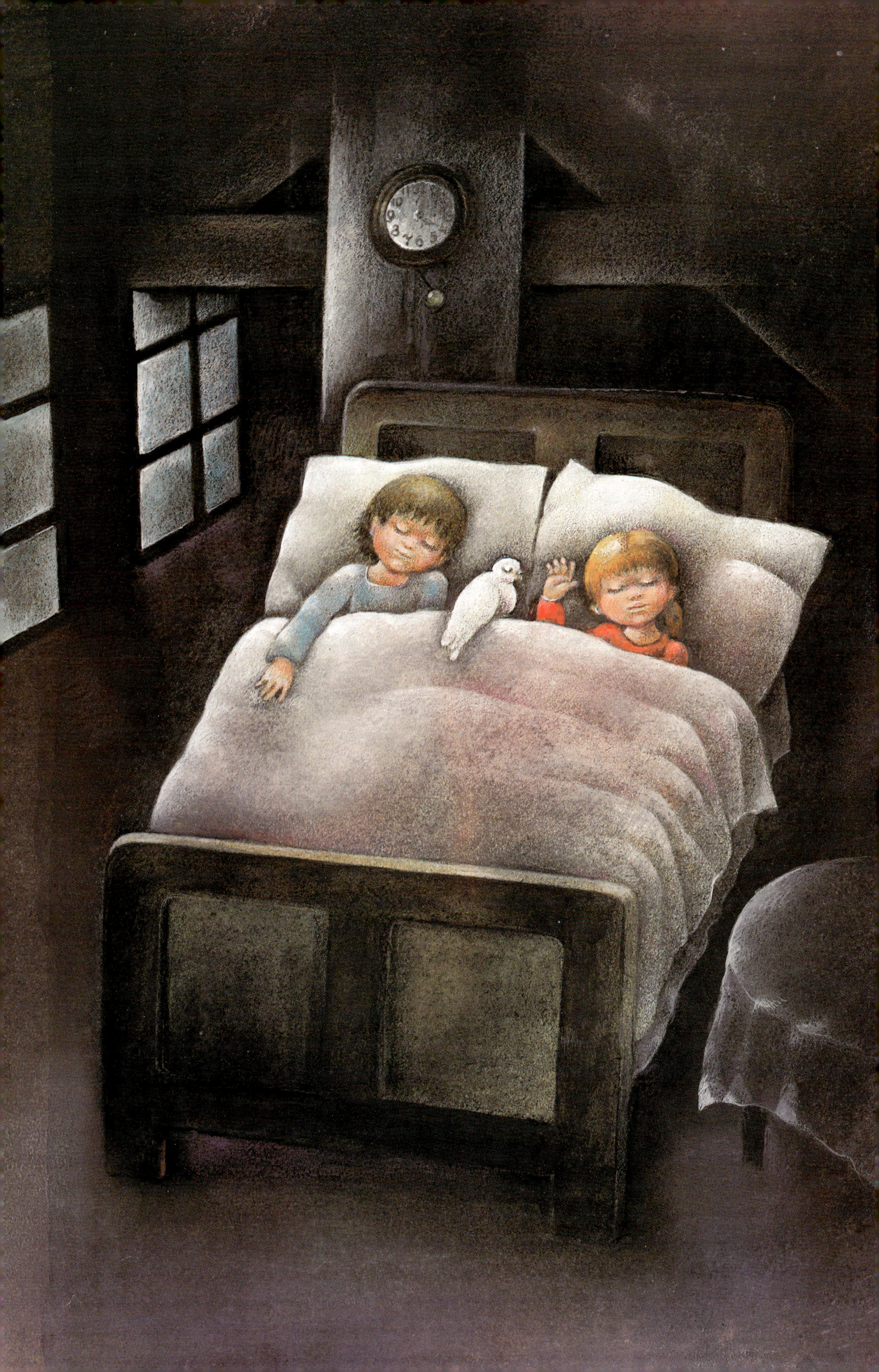

She flew strongly after her night's rest and food and soon the grey-gold plains began to slip away behind her. Suddenly, a shadow crossed the sun. She glanced behind her: it was a hawk! Desperately, she twisted and turned, dodging the terrible claws which stretched out to seize her. Then, as she dived into the trees, a shout rang out and the hawk paused for an instant in surprise.

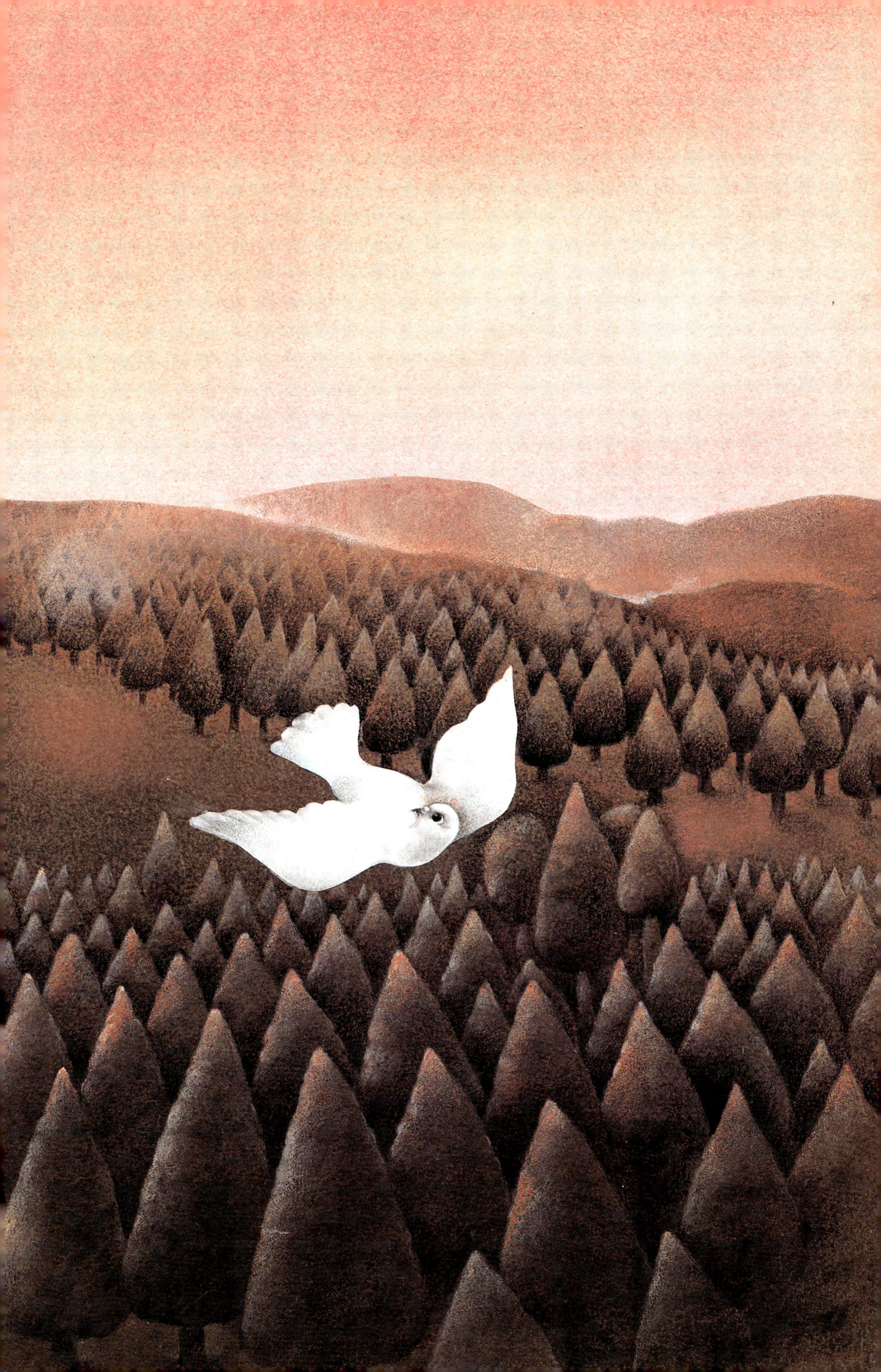

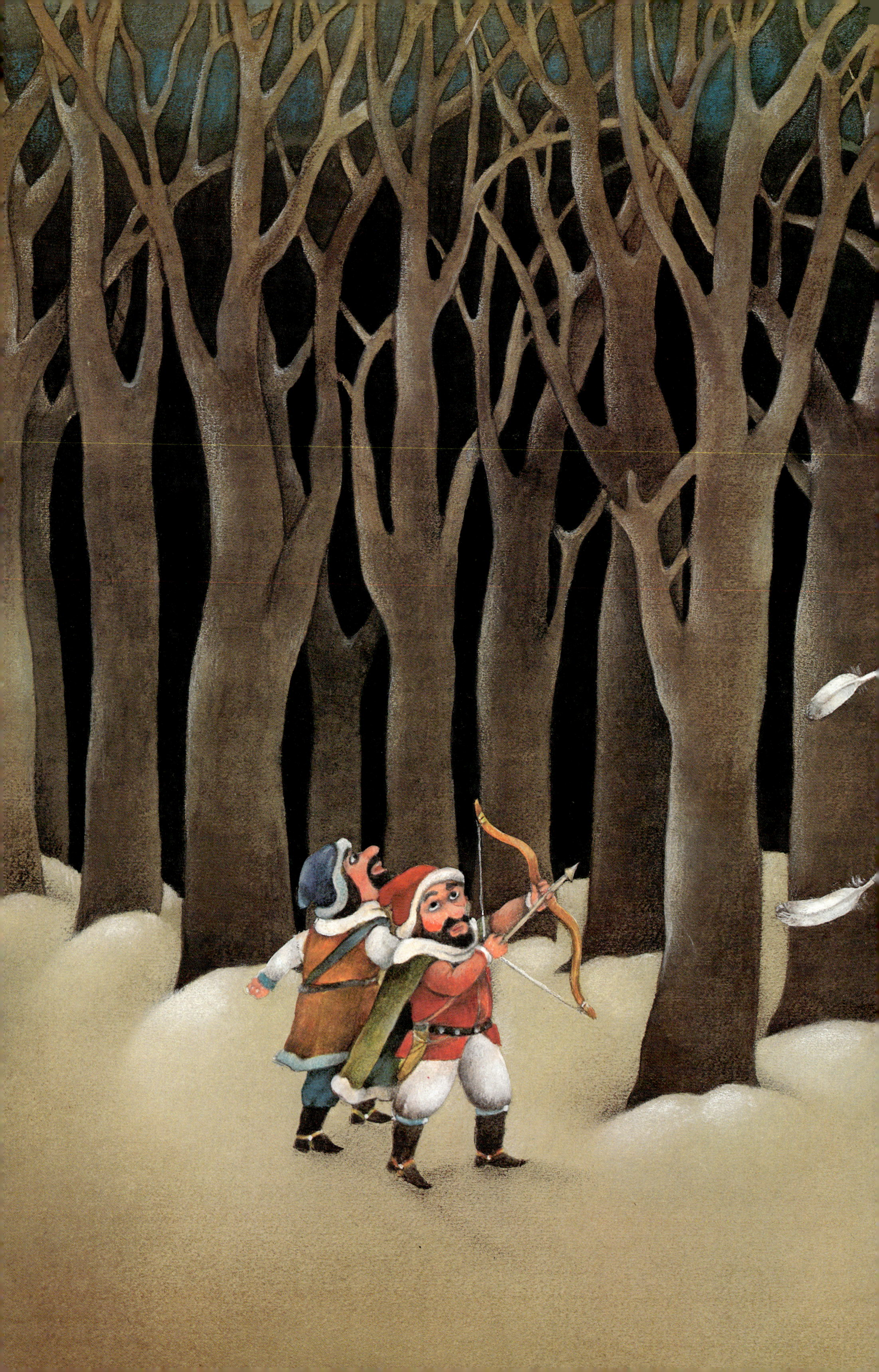

'Look at that beautiful dove!' came the hunter's cry. 'We've saved it from the hawk. Let's kill it ourselves.'

His friend drew back his bow and the dove heard the twang of the bowstring. An arrow hummed past and a couple of white feathers floated to the ground. Once again, she had escaped to continue her journey.

That night she slept in the forest and early on the morning of the seventh day she continued her journey. All day she flew and everywhere she could see signs of the coming war.

The sun had already set when she saw the palace which had once been her home. Was she in time? Would the king read her message?

She landed at the window of the king's room and tapped with her beak. The king was working on plans for war as he rose to let her in. The dove perched on his shoulder and nuzzled his ear with her beak, just as she used to do before he had been made king. Puzzled, he untied the message round her leg and read it. Then he looked hard at the dove, resting quietly after her terrible journey, and he felt suddenly very ashamed of himself.

'You are my very own white dove,' he said, quietly. 'No bird is swifter and you have always been with me in times of trouble. You brought the news of my father's death and now you are here to stop my stupidity.'

He called for his ministers. 'Listen,' he said, 'there shall be no war. Why should we fight with our friends over a name? Great or small, it is by our actions that we should be judged, not our names.

'I shall go on a visit to my wise neighbour to ask for his forgiveness and, so that the dove's journey is remembered, the new flag of our country shall be the white dove of peace.'

Copyright © Bohem Press 1987

Copyright © English translation Hutchinson Children's Books 1988

All rights reserved

First published in Great Britain in 1988 by Hutchinson Children's Books
An imprint of Century Hutchinson Ltd
Brookmount House, 62–65 Chandos Place, Covent Garden
London WC2N 4NW

Century Hutchinson Australia Pty Ltd
16–22 Church Street, Hawthorn, Melbourne, Victoria 3122

Century Hutchinson New Zealand Limited
32–34 View Road, PO Box 40–086, Glenfield, Auckland 10

Century Hutchinson South Africa (Pty) Ltd
PO Box 337, Bergvlei 2012, South Africa

Set in Goudy Old Style Roman

Printed and bound in Italy

British Library Cataloguing in Publication Data

Recknagel, Friedrich
 The dove.
 I. Title II. Barankova, Vlasta III. Die
 Botschaft. *English*
 833'.914[J]   PZ7
 ISBN 0-09-173706-0